IT'S COOL TO LEARN ABOUT COUNTRIES

Social Studies Explorer

RUSSIA

◦← by Katie Marsico

CHERRY LAKE PUBLISHING • ANN ARBOR, MICHIGAN

Published in the United States of America
by Cherry Lake Publishing
Ann Arbor, Michigan
www.cherrylakepublishing.com

Content Adviser: George Gutsche, PhD, Professor of Russian and Slavic Studies,
The University of Arizona

Book design: The Design Lab

Photo credits: Cover, ©Lloid/Shutterstock, Inc.; cover and pages 3, 8, 20 top, 21 top, 26 top, 31
top, 34 top, 44 top, and 48, ©iStockphoto.com/michaelgzc; cover and pages 7 bottom, 23, 26
bottom, 34 bottom, and 41 bottom, ©iStockphoto.com/bluestocking; page 4, ©iStockphoto.com/
AlexKhrom; page 6, ©Vera Volkova/Shutterstock, Inc.; page 7 top, ©Mcseem/Dreamstime.com; page
9, ©Razumovskaya Marina Nikolaevna/Shutterstock, Inc.; page 12, ©Yuckinus/Dreamstime.com;
page 13, ©iStockphoto.com/Mordolff; page 14, ©Egorov1976/Dreamstime.com; page 15 top, ©Kitch
Bain/Shutterstock, Inc.; page 15 bottom, ©iStockphoto.com/opulent-images; page 16, ©iStockphoto.
com/SGV; page 17, ©Classic Image/Alamy; page 18, ©RIA Novosti/Alamy; page 19, ©Markwaters/
Dreamstime.com; page 21 bottom, ©iStockphoto.com/Mik122; page 24, ©Soloir/Dreamstime.com;
page 25, ©NORMA JOSEPH/Alamy; page 28, ©Andrey Kekyalyaynen/Alamy; pages 29 and 30,
©Dimaberkut/Dreamstime.com; page 31 bottom, ©vanille/Shutterstock, Inc.; page 32, ©Avatavat/
Dreamstime.com; page 33, ©Oleksiy Maksymenko/Alamy; page 35, ©huntsman/Shutterstock,
Inc.; page 36, ©Scott Rothstein/Shutterstock, Inc.; page 39, ©Id1974/Dreamstime.com; page 40,
©Elzbieta Sekowska/Shutterstock, Inc.; page 41 top, ©Vladimirs Koskins/Shutterstock, Inc.; page
42, ©iStockphoto.com/tazytaz; page 44 bottom, ©Nayashkova Olga/Shutterstock, Inc.; page 45,
©Bratwustle/Shutterstock, Inc.

Library of Congress Cataloging-in-Publication Data
Marsico, Katie, 1980-
  It's cool to learn about countries: Russia/by Katie Marsico.
      p. cm.—(Social studies explorer)
  Includes bibliographical references and index.
  ISBN-13: 978-1-60279-831-1 (lib. bdg.)
  ISBN-10: 1-60279-831-1 (lib. bdg.)
1. Russia (Federation)—Juvenile literature. I. Title. II. Title: Russia. III. Series.
  DK510.23.M37 2011
  947—dc22   2009049451

Cherry Lake Publishing would like to acknowledge the work of The Partnership for 21st Century
Skills. Please visit www.21stcenturyskills.org for more information.

Printed in the United States of America
Corporate Graphics Inc.
July 2010
CLFA07

TABLE OF CONTENTS

CHAPTER ONE
Welcome to Russia! 4

CHAPTER TWO
Business and Government in Russia 16

CHAPTER THREE
Meet the People 25

CHAPTER FOUR
Celebrations 32

CHAPTER FIVE
What's for Dinner? 40

Glossary 46
For More Information 47
Index 48
About the Author 48

WELCOME TO RUSSIA!

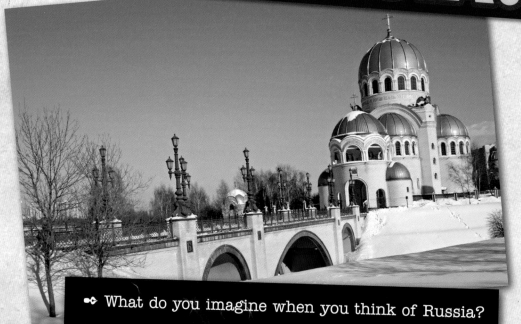

⊷ What do you imagine when you think of Russia?

Would you like to explore Russia? It is the largest country in the world. More than 140 million people live there. No matter what part of the nation you visit, you'll discover a country that is rich in unique foods, celebrations, and traditions.

What type of geography do you imagine when you think of Russia? If you picture frosty treeless plains,

you would be right! But that is only one example of Russian geography.

The nation spans two continents: Europe and Asia. It features a wide variety of land formations. Russia measures 6,601,668 square miles (17,098,242 square kilometers). It is bordered by the Arctic Ocean to the north. China, Mongolia, and Kazakhstan are found to the south. The North Pacific Ocean is to the east of Russia. The Caspian, Black, and Baltic Seas and the Caucasus Mountains lie along its western boundary. So do Scandinavia and various Eastern European countries.

Russia is located south of the Arctic Ocean and to the north of China, Mongolia, and Kazakhstan.

Russia is a **federation** consisting of 83 territories and regions. Each one is represented in the national government. Moscow is the nation's capital and largest city. It is situated in western Russia. St. Petersburg, which ranks second in size to Moscow, is just to the north. These cities are west of the Ural Mountains. The portion of the country in which they are located is filled with broad plains, low hills, and several forests.

East of the Urals, which divide Europe and Asia, lies Siberia. This region forms much of the central and eastern portion of Russia. It occupies about 75 percent of Russia's landmass. Northern Siberia is famous for its tundra. Only certain shrubs and grasses are able to push their way upward through the frosty soil there.

Russia is often described as a land of extremes. Consider the Kamchatka Peninsula, which is located between the Bering Sea and the Sea of Okhotsk. A peninsula is a strip of land that juts out into a body of water. Kamchatka is sometimes referred to as a land of fire and ice. It is the site of hot springs and active volcanoes as well as snowy mountains and freezing temperatures.

The Russian taiga is found just south of the tundra. It stretches from the Urals to the Pacific. It contains massive **coniferous** forests. Treeless grasslands and plains called steppes are located south of the taiga. These areas are better for farming than the tundra and taiga and are often used to grow wheat. The soil can be extremely dry, though.

Do you want to climb the tallest mountain in Russia? Head to the Caucasus in the southwestern part of the country. Mount Elbrus is Russia's highest point and stretches 18,510 feet (5,642 meters) toward the sky.

➦ Lake Baikal is one of Russia's most impressive landmarks.

Several mountain ranges zigzag across southern and eastern Russia. They include the Sayan, Kolyma, Stanovoy, Verkhoyansk, and Cherskiy ranges. Countless rivers, lakes, and seas also shape the country's landscape. Lake Ladoga in situated in the north. It is the largest lake in Europe. Lake Baikal in southern Siberia holds approximately 20 percent of the world's fresh surface water. It is believed to be between 25 million and 30 million years old, making it the planet's oldest lake.

Take a close look at this map of Russia. Trace the outline of the country on a separate sheet of paper. Draw a star to mark where Moscow is located. Find an atlas or locate

Arctic Ocean

RUSSIA

CHINA

JAPAN

MONGOLIA

a map of Russia online. Then sketch some of the nation's many rivers, lakes, and mountain ranges. Does your map reflect Russia's many geographic features?

How should you dress if you plan to visit Russia? If you head to the Siberian tundra, be sure to pack a heavy coat! In the winter, temperatures can drop to well below freezing.

❖ You don't want to be caught outside in the icy winds of the Siberian tundra!

•➤ Moscow's weather is often pleasant during the summer.

In fact, the average yearly temperature throughout most of Russia is freezing or below freezing. That does not mean you will never have the opportunity to wear shorts or sandals. In Moscow, for example, temperatures often climb to approximately 86 degrees Fahrenheit (30 degrees Celsius) in the summer.

● Sunflowers can grow to become very large.

Is it possible for anything to survive in portions of the country where the climate is at its most extreme? Absolutely! Russia is home to an incredible variety of plants and animals, even on the tundra. Organisms called lichens are a combination of algae and fungi and grow in the nation's northernmost regions. Bright sunflowers bloom in milder areas to the south and west. Russia is recognized as the world's largest producer of sunflowers.

Several of the country's animal species, sadly, are **endangered**. Two examples are snow leopards and sea otters. Do not forget to look for these creatures as you explore Russia!

snow leopard

sea otter

CHAPTER TWO

BUSINESS AND GOVERNMENT IN RUSSIA

➥ Oil production is an important part of the Russian economy.

Russia traces its roots to an earlier Eastern **Slavic** state formed in the late 9th century. By the 18th century, Russia had become large and powerful enough to be called the Russian Empire. The economy and system of government have undergone many changes through the past several decades.

Until the early 1900s, emperors called czars controlled the nation. In 1917, revolutionaries overthrew Czar Nicholas II and ultimately executed him and his family. For most of the remaining century, Russia was known as the Union of Soviet Socialist Republics. It was more commonly referred to as the U.S.S.R. or Soviet Union. The people lived under **Communist** rule. The term *Communism* (with a capital "C") often refers to a specific type of economic system. In this system, the state owns property and determines how work is performed. The state also decides how the products of that work are shared.

Czar Nicholas II was the ruler of Russia for more than 20 years.

Former Soviet president Mikhail Gorbachev won the Nobel Peace Prize in 1990.

As time passed, citizens of the Soviet Union became eager for more freedoms and a greater voice in government. They also wanted a better supply of goods and food. In 1985, Mikhail Gorbachev became leader of the Communist Party. He pushed for changes in the economy and government. These reforms led to changes in other parts of Eastern Europe. By the end of 1991, the Soviet Union and its Communist system had collapsed.

In the early 1990s, the current Russian Federation was formed. It consists of a union of 83 individual territories and regions. They are all joined together under a central government. The federation features a president who is elected by the people and serves as chief of state. He or she appoints and works closely with a premier, or prime minister. This person is often described as the actual head of government. Along with other ministers, these officials are at the center of Russia's executive branch. This area of government is responsible for ensuring that the nation's laws are carried out.

President Dmitry Medvedev was elected in 2008. Vladimir Putin took office as premier that same year. Putin also served as the nation's president from 2000 to 2008.

Dmitry Medvedev

Russia's legislative branch is represented by the Federal Assembly. This lawmaking body includes two houses—the Federation Council and the State Duma. The government also has a judicial branch that makes important decisions related to the country's laws.

The current Russian flag was adopted in 1991. It features three horizontal stripes of the same length and width. The top stripe is white, the middle one is blue, and the bottom stripe is red.

As a result of the many changes that have taken place in Russia, its economic system is still developing. Experts often describe the nation as having a market economy. This means that the actions of consumers and privately owned companies are the biggest factors that affect business.

The ruble is Russia's standard currency. It can take the form of both paper money and coins. In 2010, one U.S. dollar equaled approximately 29.5 Russian rubles.

In 2008, more than 75 million men and women made up Russia's labor force. What type of work do they do? Some work for companies that supplied the approximately $472 billion in **exports** that were shipped out of Russia that same year. Such goods include petroleum, natural gas, and a variety of metals and chemicals.

Do you want to know more about Russia's economy? Then take a look at its trading partners. Trading partners are the countries that **import** goods from a country or export goods to that country. Here is a graph showing the countries that are Russia's top import and export trading partners.

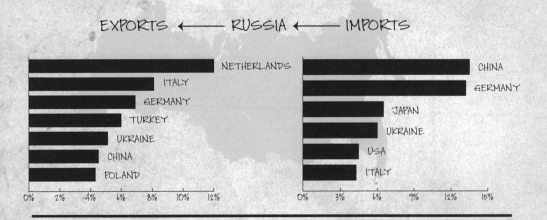

EXPORTS ← RUSSIA ← IMPORTS

Services represent approximately 58 percent of the nation's business activity. An example of a service is the education that teachers provide. More than 37 percent of Russia's business is connected to manufacturing. People who have manufacturing jobs produce goods for sale. Russian companies are involved in the production of coal, oil, gas, and chemicals. They also produce metals and transportation and farm equipment. Agriculture makes up nearly 5 percent of the country's business activity. Farmers often grow sunflowers, potatoes, and beets. Wheat and other grains are grown, too. Farmers also raise beef and dairy cattle.

Work is only one aspect of Russian life. Do you want to learn more about the men, women, and children who call Russia home?

•➤ Agriculture is especially important to people who live in Russia's rural areas.

In 2007, approximately 10 percent of Russia's workers had jobs related to agriculture. Another 27 percent were employed in careers connected to manufacturing. Slightly more than 62 percent worked in service-related fields.

Use this information to create a bar graph that represents these sections of Russia's labor force. Ask an adult for help if you need it. Which bar do you predict will be the longest? Which do you think will be the shortest?

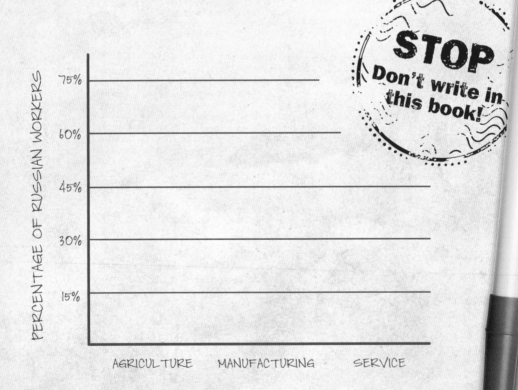

STOP
Don't write in this book!

CHAPTER THREE

MEET THE PEOPLE

➥ Russia's population is made up of people from a diverse range of cultural backgrounds.

In 2009, Russian officials indicated that 140,041,247 people lived within their country's borders. The year before, they noted that 73 percent of the people had homes in **urban** areas. This means that they were residents of major cities such as Moscow and St. Petersburg as well as neighboring suburbs.

Most Russians live in the European portion of the country. This is the region west of the Ural Mountains.

Several different cultural groups exist throughout the nation. Nearly 80 percent of the population are native Russians. Together, the Tatar, Bashkir, and Chuvash ethnic groups make up more than 6 percent. Another 2 percent of people living in Russia are originally from Ukraine. The remaining 12 percent either do not specify their background or claim a different ethnicity.

What is the main language these individuals speak? Russian! This is a Slavic language. Have you ever seen a sign that was written in Russian? The letters probably did not look the same as the ones you are familiar with. People who write in Russian use the Cyrillic alphabet. Cyrillic letters are partly based on the Greek alphabet, while English letters are linked to the Roman alphabet.

RUSSIAN

Try writing a few letters of the Cyrillic alphabet. The letters in the left-hand column are part of the Roman alphabet. Those to the right are Cyrillic. On a separate sheet of paper, match the Roman letters to their Cyrillic counterparts. See the answers below. Then practice writing the Cyrillic letters you have learned.

Roman alphabet
1. b
2. d
3. f
4. g

Cyrillic alphabet
1. Ф
2. Б
3. Г
4. Д

STOP
Don't write in this book!

Answers: 1-2; 2-4; 3-1; 4-3

◦◦ If you lived in Russia, you would probably have the same classmates every year.

Younger students in Russia practice their reading and writing skills when they begin school. Everyone from the age of seven until the late teens must attend classes. Most students take advantage of Russia's public schools, which are free. Some are enrolled at private institutions.

From age 7 onward, the majority of Russian children are placed in groups of 25 to 30 students. These groups generally remain the same for the next several years.

When they turn 16, students have the option of transferring out of their regular secondary schools to attend training institutions. There, they learn specialized skills that prepare them for certain careers.

Students ages 18 and older who have successfully completed their educational requirements may enroll in classes at the university level. Some young people choose to attend colleges and universities in other countries.

➥ Some Russian students go on to medical school after they finish their educational requirements.

Like education, religion is very important to many Russians. The majority of Russians, about 70 percent, identify themselves as members of the Russian Orthodox Church. A small percentage of Russians are members of other Christian religions. Roughly 10 to 15 percent of Russia's citizens are Muslim and believe in the teachings of Islam. A small percentage of residents practice the Jewish faith.

➥ The Russian Orthodox religion is a major part of Russian culture and society.

Have you ever seen a Russian Orthodox cathedral? Look no further than Moscow or St. Petersburg! These areas are filled with churches that feature colorful onion domes. Russia is often associated with these pointed, bulb-shaped domes.

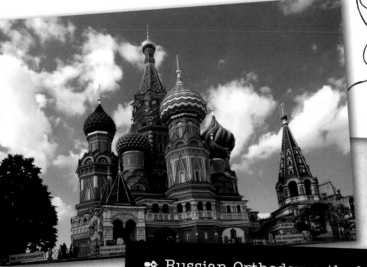

➜ Russian Orthodox cathedrals feature colorful domes.

Religion is related to several of the nation's cultural traditions and celebrations. Get ready to discover how Russians celebrate!

CHAPTER FOUR

CELEBRATIONS

◆ Many Russian celebrations feature music and dancing.

Russians have countless ways of celebrating their cultural traditions, beliefs, and personal interests. One way involves playing games. Many Russians also use holiday festivities to express their religious views or pride in their national history.

What is your favorite pastime? If your answer involves a sport, you have a lot in common with people in Russia. Soccer, ice hockey, and basketball are all popular in that country. Many Russians also enjoy ice skating, playing chess, and sharing folktales.

Baba Yaga is a popular figure in many Russian folktales. This character is sometimes depicted as an evil witch. In other cases, she is described as a wise old woman. Her house sits atop chicken legs. There is usually a lesson or moral in stories about Baba Yaga.

Baba Yaga

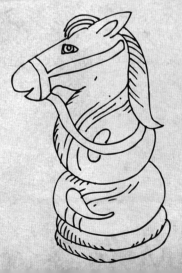

Holiday festivities are another way of celebrating Russian culture. Many of these events occur in the winter. Russians who practice Christianity celebrate Christmas. In Russia, this falls on January 7. December 25 is the common date in other parts of the world. This is because the Russian Orthodox Church uses the **Julian calendar** to plan its holidays. Most other Christian groups follow the **Gregorian calendar** instead.

Russians often celebrate seasonal holidays during a special Winter Festival. It is held from December 25 through January 5. People across the country come together to enjoy folk music concerts and traditional foods. They also await the arrival of Father Frost. He is similar to the holiday character that many children call Santa Claus. Along with his granddaughter, Snow Maiden, he hands out gifts to Russian children.

•❖ Russians often put up beautiful decorations for winter holidays such as Christmas and New Year's Eve.

Russians often consider New Year's to be a bigger holiday than Christmas. They gather with friends and family to eat huge meals, sing carols, give gifts, and watch fireworks.

A popular springtime holiday is Easter. This is an opportunity for Christians to celebrate their belief that Jesus Christ rose from the dead. The exact date of Russian Easter varies each year. Many enjoy a special dessert called paskha. This dish is similar to cheesecake. Members of the Christian faith also typically attend church services and decorate eggs.

CRAFT ACTIVITY

When the czars ruled Russia, members of the royal family often exchanged Fabergé eggs at Easter. These jeweled creations are made of precious metals and gemstones. They have since come to represent luxury and wealth. Would you like to make your own Fabergé eggs?

❧ Some people still collect Fabergé eggs.

MATERIALS:
- Pencil
- Scissors
- Glue
- Sequins
- Construction paper (multiple colors)
- Crayons or markers
- Glitter
- Stickers

INSTRUCTIONS:

1. Use a pencil to trace a large, oval-shaped outline of an egg on a sheet of construction paper.
2. Cut out your egg using scissors. Lay the cutout on a clean, flat surface.

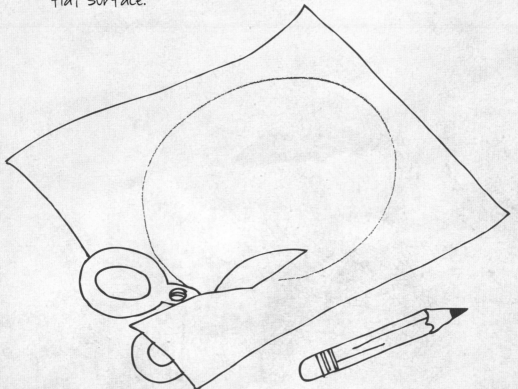

Continued on the following page →

3. Decide how you want to decorate the egg. Remember that real Fabergé eggs sparkle with precious metals and jewels. They also feature detailed designs. Use crayons or markers to sketch diamonds and other gems on your paper egg. Glue glitter and shiny sequins to your egg in creative designs. You could use stickers, too.
4. Allow the glue to dry completely.

   Make several Fabergé eggs. Then give them to friends and family members as special springtime gifts.

➡ Parades are a traditional part of Victory Day celebrations.

Other Russian holidays include Victory Day, which falls on May 9. This is a celebration of the country's triumph over enemy forces during World War II (1939–1945). On June 12, Russians observe Russia Day. This holiday marks when the Russian legislature declared Russia's independence from Soviet control.

CHAPTER FIVE

WHAT'S FOR DINNER?

❖ Blini are sometimes topped with fish eggs, known as caviar.

Do you like pancakes? You should try blini. These are Russian pancakes that can be eaten plain. They can also be rolled around fillings such as chocolate syrup, jams, cheeses, or meats. Russian **cuisine** features many other dishes, too.

Samovar

Do you have a teapot in your kitchen? Many people in Russia use electric kettles. But you might find traditional samovars there, too. These metal urns are used to boil water for tea. Tea is the favorite beverage of many Russians. Samovars are often made from copper, bronze, silver, or iron. They sometimes feature elaborate engravings or beautiful paintings.

Meals in this country generally feature hearty dishes. Russians often use vegetables such as beets, mushrooms, potatoes, and cabbage in their cooking. Meats, including beef, chicken, fish, and pork, are also an important part of the diet. So is bread. It is frequently served with cheese or sweet jams at mealtime. Sour cream and butter are added to many dishes, too.

Tea is a popular drink in Russia. How about preparing a pot of Russian tea? This recipe requires using a stove to heat the ingredients. Ask an adult to help you.

Russian Tea

INGREDIENTS

6 cups (1.4 liters) cold water

1 cinnamon stick

6 whole cloves

4 decaffeinated black tea bags

1 cup (236.6 milliliters) orange juice

2 tablespoons (29.6 ml) lemon juice

¼ cup (47.9 grams) sugar

½ teaspoon (1.3 g) grated nutmeg

INSTRUCTIONS

1. Combine the water, cinnamon, and cloves in a saucepan.
2. Have an adult bring these ingredients to a boil on the stove.
3. Carefully remove the saucepan from the heat. Drop in the tea bags. Allow them to steep, or soak in the water, for 5 minutes.
4. Use a slotted spoon to remove the tea bags, cinnamon, and cloves.
5. Mix the orange juice, lemon juice, sugar, and nutmeg in a separate saucepan. Have an adult heat these ingredients until the sugar dissolves.
6. Add this mixture to your tea. Ask an adult to reheat the tea and juice mixture if it becomes too cool at this point.

Carefully pour your tea into mugs or teacups and enjoy!

What are some other foods that would typically be served in Russia? Many residents enjoy borscht, or beet soup. They also like ikra, which is commonly referred to as caviar. This delicacy is made of salted fish eggs. Ikra is often served with dark, crusty bread or blini.

Soup is not always served piping hot in Russia. In fact, residents often serve certain soups cold. When serving a soup called botvinya, many Russians place crushed ice in the bowl so the broth stays cool.

3 ст

Н Р БЪЛГАРИЯ

•● Borscht can be served either hot or cold.

Pirozhki and pelmeni are also popular Russian foods. Pirozhki are pastries that contain meat, cabbage, potatoes, or cheese. Pelmeni are meatball dumplings.

What about dessert? You have already read about paskha, which is traditionally served at Easter. Teacakes coated in powdered sugar are popular. Pastries, breads, and cookies made with honey and walnuts are other favorites.

Has Russia captured your imagination yet? You could spend years taking in all the sights that this huge nation has to offer. Which part of Russia will you explore next?

➦ Pirozhki come in many different flavors. Each one is delicious in its own way!

GLOSSARY

Communist (KOM-yuh-nist) having to do with a type of government with an economy that is based on public or state control of property and business

coniferous (ko-NIF-uh-ruhss) having to do with evergreen trees that produce cones

cuisine (kwi-ZEEN) a style or way of cooking or presenting food

endangered (en-DAYN-jurd) at risk of dying out completely

exports (EK-sportss) acts of selling something to another country or products sold in this way

federation (fed-uh-RAY-shuhn) a collection of territories and regions that are represented by a central government or joined together by some type of agreement

Gregorian calendar (gri-GOR-ee-uhn KAL-uhn-dur) a calendar system used by much of the international world

import (IM-port) bring in from another country

Julian calendar (JOO-lee-uhn KAL-uhn-dur) a calendar system used by certain countries and religions

Slavic (SLAH-vik) having to do with a family of languages that includes Russian, Polish, and others or with a speaker of those languages

urban (UR-buhn) having to do with cities

FOR MORE INFORMATION

Books

Russell, Henry. *Russia*. Washington, DC: National Geographic, 2008.

Schemenauer, Elma. *Welcome to Russia*. Mankato, MN: Child's World, 2008.

Streissguth, Thomas. *Russia*. Minneapolis: Lerner Publications, 2008.

Web Sites

Central Intelligence Agency—The World Factbook: Russia
www.cia.gov/library/publications/the-world-factbook/geos/rs.html
Check out this site for information about Russia's economy, geography, population, and government.

National Geographic Kids—Russia
kids.nationalgeographic.com/Places/Find/Russia
Scan this site for an overview of Russia, from geographic information to cultural highlights.

TIME for Kids—Russia
www.timeforkids.com/TFK/kids/hh/goplaces/main/0,28375,595847,00.html
You'll find information about Russian history and more at this helpful site.

activities, 10–11, 24, 36–38, 42–43
agriculture, 8, 23, 24
animals, 14, 15, 23
Arctic Ocean, 5
Asian continent, 5, 7

Baba Yaga, 33
Baltic Sea, 5
Black Sea, 5
blini (pancakes), 40
borders, 5

calendars, 34
capital city, 6
Caspian Sea, 5
Caucasus Mountains, 5, 8
caviar, 44
cities, 6, 25
climate, 7, 12–14
Communism, 17, 18
coniferous forests, 8
Cyrillic alphabet, 27
czars, 17, 36

economy, 16, 17, 18, 21, 22
education, 23, 28–29
elections, 19
elevation, 8
endangered species, 15
ethnic groups, 26–27
European continent, 5, 7, 26
executive branch of government, 19
exports, 22

Fabergé eggs, 36–38
Federal Assembly, 20
Federation Council, 20
flag, 20
folktales, 33
foods, 18, 34, 40–41, 42–43, 44–45
forests, 6, 8

Gorbachev, Mikhail, 18

holidays, 32, 34–35, 39

industries, 23, 24

jobs, 22, 23, 24
judicial branch of government, 20

Kamchatka Peninsula, 7

lakes, 9
land area, 5
languages, 27
laws, 19, 20
legislative branch of government, 20, 39

maps, 5, 10–11
market economies, 21
Medvedev, Dmitry, 19
money, 21
Moscow, 6, 10, 13, 25, 31
mountains, 5, 7, 8, 9, 26
Mount Elbrus, 8

Nicholas II (czar), 17
North Pacific Ocean, 5

paskha (dessert), 45
pelmeni (dumplings), 45
pirozhki (pastry), 45
plants, 7, 8, 14
population, 4, 25
premiers, 19
presidents, 19
Putin, Vladimir, 19

regions, 6, 7, 14, 19
religion, 30–31, 32, 34, 35
rubles (money), 21
Russian Empire, 16
Russian Federation, 6, 19
Russian Orthodox Church, 30, 31, 34

samovars (teapots), 41
service industries, 23, 24
Siberia, 7, 9, 12
Slavic language, 27
Slavic states, 16
soups, 44
Soviet Union, 17–18, 39
sports, 33
State Duma, 20
steppes, 8
St. Petersburg, 6, 25, 31
sunflowers, 14, 23

taiga, 8
tea, 41, 42–43
territories, 6, 19
trading partners, 22
tundra, 7, 8, 12, 14

Ural Mountains, 6, 7, 8, 26

volcanoes, 7

Winter Festival, 34

ABOUT THE AUTHOR
Katie Marsico has written more than 60 books for young readers. She has never visited Russia, but one of her ancestors fought in the czar's army during the 19th century.